Love Letters from OUR GOD and to OUR GOD

JUANITA WILSON

ISBN 979-8-88943-830-4 (paperback)
ISBN 979-8-88943-831-1 (digital)

Christian Faith Publishing
832 Park Avenue
Meadville, PA 16335
www.christianfaithpublishing.com

Printed in the United States of America

Contents

Foreword v

The Restoration of God 1

Jesus Is Our Heaven 3

Lord, Will You Marry Me? 5

A Heaven of a Man 7

Thank You, God, for the Part of You That Lives Inside of Me 8

There Is a Man in the House 9

The Hope of the Resurrection 10

Today, Jesus Was Passing By 12

The Secret Message 13

There Is a Love That Can Not Be Broken 15

This Is Real love 17

The Morning Light 19

An Everlasting Power and Love 20

We Live to Live Again 22

My Beloved 24

Love Is Always Here 26

God Has Given His Promise and His Oath 28

Because of the Jesus Who Lives in Me 30

See Your Life through God's Eyes 31

You Forgave 33

Unto Us 34

Our God's Grace 35

Please Forgive Me 36

You Must Pay Attention 37

A Man of Complete Integrity 38

Am I Not Worthy of Your Praise? 39

You Already Have It 41

Let Us Do Something New 43

To Kiss Our King 44

All You Have to Do Is Reach for Him 46

There Is a Man in the House 47

Last Night, Jesus Woke Me Up 48

I Have Chosen This Temple 50

Thank You for Bringing Me Back 51

My Perfect Father 52

A Brief Moment 54

I Come to You, Lord, Because You Have My Destiny 56

God Deepest Secret 58

Women of God 59

In His Rest 61

Standing in the Shadow of God 62

When I Cry 64

Jesus, You Made Me Special 65

The Purpose of Your Life 67

Thank You for Saving Me 69

When I Die 70

Be Careful 71

You Can Unlock Your Own Door 73

Holy Spirit 75

The Eternal Life 76

Foreword

Have you ever read the Word of God and gotten an understanding of a particular scripture? Have you ever read that same scripture again and get a deeper understanding? I expect that if you read it a third time, your understanding would go deeper still. Then, there are those wonderful moments when that Word reveals an even deeper truth, and it reigns in your heart. That is the revelation knowledge we experience when, through the Word of God, the Holy Spirit brings counsel and comfort, and we begin to see the wonder and attributes of our Holy God and just how big His love is for us.

This book is a picture of the revelation knowledge the Holy Spirit unfolds to the author as she travels along her journey of a "life in Christ."

—Minister Sharon Bright

The Restoration of God

We are surrounded by the walls of God's salvation. Open the gates to all who are righteous; allow the faithful to enter. You will keep in perfect peace all who trust in You. All those thoughts are fixed on You! Trust in the Lord always, for the Lord God is the eternal rock. But for those who are righteous, the way is not steep or rough. You are a God Who does what is right, and You smooth out the path ahead of them.

Lord, we show our trust in You by obeying Your laws; our heart's desire is to glorify Your name. In the night, I searched for You; in the morning, I earnestly sought You. For only when You come to judge, the earth will people learn what is right. Your kindness to the wicked does not make them do good. Although others do right, the wicked keep doing wrong and take no notice of the Lord's majesty. Show them Your eagerness to defend Your people. Then they will be ashamed.

Lord, You will grant us peace; all we have accomplished is really from You. Oh Lord, You have made our nation great; yes, You have made us great. We have extended our borders, and we give You the glory. We pray beneath the burdens of Your discipline. So were we in Your presence, Lord. We have not given salvation to the earth nor brought fife into the world. But those who die in the Lord will live; their bodies will rise again! Those who sleep on the earth will rise and sing for joy! For Your life-giving light will fall like dew on Your people in the place of the dead. They will be brought out for all to see.

Reverence to the Lord is pure and lasts forever. The laws of the Lord are true; each one is fair. How can I know all the sins lurking in my heart? Cleanse me from these hidden faults. Keep Your servant from deliberate sin! Don't let them control me. Then I will be free of guilt, innocent of great sin. May the words of my mouth and the meditation of my heart be pleasing to You, O Lord, my rock and my redeemer.

Love, Sugar
Ms. Juanita Wilson

Jesus Is Our Heaven

The Bible tells us that God is in everything. And if God is in everything, He is in heaven too. So are You in heaven, Lord? That is so amazing to even imagine that our God is in heaven. Heaven walked on this earth just like you and me. Our God is so great. He is greater than anything in this world. He can be there in heaven, and He can be on earth at the same time. That is how great our God is.

Heaven will answer a prayer. Thank You, God. Heaven loves us more than anything. Joyful are people of integrity who follow the instructions of the Lord. Joyful of those who obey his laws and search for Him with all their hearts. They do not compromise with evil, and they walk only in His path. Then I will not be ashamed when I compare my life with Your command. As I learn Your righteous regulations, I will thank You by living as I should! Lord, please don't give up on me! I have hidden Your Word in my heart so that I might not sin against You.

Lord, be good to Your servant so that I may live and obey Your Word. Open my eyes to see the wonderful truths in Your instructions. I am only a foreigner in the land. I lie in the dust; revive me by Your Word. Help me understand the meaning of Your commandments. I will meditate on Your wonderful deeds. I weep with sorrow; encourage me with Your Word. Keep me from lying to myself; give me the privilege of knowing Your instructions. I have chosen to be faithful; I have determined to live by Your regulations. I cling to Your laws, Lord. Don't let me put You to shame! I will pursue Your commandments, for You expand my understanding. Lord, give me Your unfailing love and salvation that You promised me. Do not snatch Your Word of truth from me, for Your regulations are my only hope. I will walk in freedom, for I have devoted myself to Your commandments. Remember Your promise to me; it is my only hope. It comforts me in all of my troubles.

Your decrees have been the theme of my songs wherever I have lived. Lord, You are mine, and I am Yours. Be merciful, as You promised. Thank You, my Lord.

I am Yours,
Ms. JUANITA WILSON

Lord, Will You Marry Me?

Lord, You have been with me before the beginning of time. You were there when I was born dead. And You are the one Who breathed into me to give me life.

Lord, will You marry me? You were there with me in my childhood, and You took care of me when bad things were happening all around me. You were there when a man climbed through my window to go get something to eat, and then he climbed back out the same window, and You were there with me.

Lord, will You marry me? You were there when someone touched me who should not have touched me. You were there when I was raped, and I was able to walk away. You were there when I was hungry and someone knocked on my door. He came because of You, Lord. You were there when I didn't have anywhere to live, and You made a way out of no way for me and my children. Thank You, Lord.

Lord, will You marry me? You were there when I died twice having a child, and I am still here, my Lord. You were with me when I had my heart attack, and I died again. Someone who loved me came and said a prayer just for me, and I am still here. You let me have another heart attack, and I didn't even know it. That is how good You have been to me. Lord, I want to thank You. Lord, will You marry me?

There is this amazing love that has been waiting on you all your life. Please don't miss the greatest love of your life because you don't believe that He is real. He has always been your God. He is still your God, and He will always be your God. No matter what happens in this life, He is always there.

LORD, YOU HAVE ALWAYS BEEN WITH ME. ALWAYS AND FOREVER. LORD, WILL YOU MARRY ME?

THE LORD KEEPS WATCH OVER YOU AS YOU COME AND GO. BOTH NOW AND FOREVER, AMEN.

LOVE,
SUGAR
Ms. JUANITA WILSON

A Heaven of a Man

When the mess is all out
And your new life begins
When life gets better
And when you don't have to look back
When you can look ahead but cannot see
And you still can believe, that your God loves you.
When you can stop listening to the wrong voice
And start listening to your God.
When you can get out of your own way and be thankful
To your God Who has loved and protected you forever
When the light comes on and you finally get it
And you start to cry because you get a chance
To start all over again because of your God
When you know that you have been forgiven
For everything you have done wrong. And He still loves you.
When you can ask for forgiveness, and He
will. Because He has always been
your God and He will always be your God,
and He will never change His mind
about you. When you can give your life
to Jesus is when you become a
heavenly man. Relating to heaven or the
Heavens, Divine, Sacred, And
Blessed. That is who you are meant to be
A Heaven of a Man

Love, Mama Sugar
Ms. Juanita Wilson

Thank You, God, for the Part of You That Lives Inside of Me

Thank You for being so close to me, Lord. You are so close that You know my heart, and You know my thoughts. You are so close You can feel me, Lord. You are so close that when I hurt, You hurt too. Thank You, my Lord, for being so close that I am never alone. The breath of life in me is Holy Spirit. When you breathe into me, my journey of my life begins. I thank You for being here all this time, Lord. You have led me down the right path of my life. You are so close that You go everywhere I go, Lord. Lord, I have a part of Heaven that lives inside of me. Thank You, God, for blessing me with a part of Your love, Your joy, Your peace that only You can give. You are so close that I can think about something that I need, and You have already done it. Because You are so close, I want to thank You for always being with me. I didn't have You in my life for so long that I am grateful for Your love that You have for me. I got a chance to get to know my God. You are my Father. You are my Savior. You are my best friend. Thank You for loving me so much that You gave me a part of You to live inside of me. Thank You for loving me so much that You died on the cross because You didn't want to live without me. Thank You, my Lord, for the part of You that lives inside of me. Holy Spirit, You are welcome in this place.

I love You too,
Sister Sugar
Ms. Juanita Wilson

There Is a Man in the House

There Is A Man In The House
Who Takes Care Of All My Needs
There Is A Man In The House
Who Is Always Doing Something Just For Me
There Is A Man In The House
Who I Can Talk To At Any Time
There Is A Man In This House
Who Is Always Blessing Me
There Is A Man In The House
Who Loves Me
There Is A Man In The House
Who's Always With Me
There Is A Man In The House
Who Protects Me
There Is A Man In The House
Who Saved Me
There Is A Man In The House
Who Died On The Cross Just For Me
There Is A Man In The House
And His Name Is Jesus

Love, Your daughter,
Sugar
Ms. Juanita Wilson

The Hope of the Resurrection

We urge you in the name of the Lord to live in a way that pleases God, as we have taught you. You live this way already, and we encourage you to do so even more. God's will is for you to be holy. God has called us to live holy lives. Therefore, anyone who refuses to live by these rules is not disobeying human teaching but is rejecting God, Who gives His Holy Spirit to you. For God Himself has taught you to love one another. Make it your goal to live a quiet life, mind your own business, and work with your hands. Then people who are not believers will respect the way you live, and you will not need to depend on others.

We want you to know what will happen to the believers who have died, so you will not grieve like people who have no hope. For since we believe that Jesus died and was raised to life again, we also believe that when He returns, God will bring with Him the believers who have died.

We tell you this directly from the Lord: We who are still living when the Lord returns will not meet Him ahead of those who have died. For the Lord Himself will come down from heaven with a commanding shout, with the voice of the archangel, and with the trumpet call of God. First, the believers who have died will rise from their graves. Then, together with them, we who are still alive and remain on earth will be caught up in the clouds to meet the Lord in the air. Then we will be with the Lord forever.

For you are all children of the light and of the day; we don't belong to darkness and night. So be on your guard, not asleep like the others. But let us who live in the light

Love always,
Sugar
Ms. Juanita Wilson

Today, Jesus Was Passing By

All you have to do is believe that Jesus has your back.

Stop worrying about what you can't do anything about.

Jesus will watch over you if you have faith in Him.

Just hold on to His hand and know that Jesus has you in the palm of His hand. Today, Jesus is passing by.

You need to know by faith that God will never leave you or forsake you.

He loves you that much. He has always been with you. He has never left you. You might have forgotten who He is, but He remembers who you are. You are a child of God. The Almighty God.

Today, Jesus is passing by.

Are you making Him proud of loving you? Did you say, "Good morning," to anyone today? Or, "How are you today?" Do you know how much Jesus loves you? Jesus loves you.

And have a wonderful day.

Today, Jesus is passing by.

Will He see or hear you saying something that you shouldn't be saying or acting the way that He wants you to act? Jesus is everywhere, so don't think that you are getting away with anything because you are not. Jesus is everywhere. Are you going to be doing something for Jesus when He passes by?

Love always, Sugar

The Secret Message

Chosen by the will of God to be an apostle of Jesus Christ, writing to God's holy children who are faithful brothers and sisters in Christ. May God, our Father, give you grace and peace.

For we have heard of your faith in Christ Jesus and your love for all God's people, which come from your confident hope of what God has reserved for you in heaven. You have had this expectation ever since you first heard the truth about the Good News. The same Good News that came to you is going out all over the world. It is bearing fruit everywhere by changing lives, just as it changed your lives from the day you first heard and understood the truth about God's wonderful grace. He has told us about the love for others that the Holy Spirit has given you.

We ask God to give you complete knowledge of His will and to give you spiritual wisdom and understanding. Then the way you live will always honor and please the Lord, and your lives will produce every kind of good fruit. All the while, you will grow as you learn to know God better and better. May you be filled with joy, always thanking the Father. He has enabled you to share in the inheritance that belongs to His people, who live in the light. He made peace with everything in heaven and on earth by means of Christ's blood on the cross.

This includes you, who were once far away from God. You were His enemies, separated from Him by your evil thoughts and actions. God has given me the responsibility of serving His church by proclaiming His entire message to you.

THIS MESSAGE WAS KEPT SECRET FOR CENTURIES AND GENERATIONS PAST, BUT NOW IT HAS BEEN REVEALED TO GOD'S PEOPLE. FOR GOD WANTED THEM TO KNOW THAT THE RICHES AND GLORY OF CHRIST ARE FOR YOU GENTILES TOO. AND THIS IS THE SECRET: CHRIST LIVES IN YOU. THIS GIVES YOU ASSURANCE OF SHARING HIS GLORY.

WARNING EVERYONE AND TEACHING EVERYONE WITH ALL THE WISDOM GOD HAS GIVEN US. WE WANT TO PRESENT THEM TO GOD, PERFECT IN THEIR RELATIONSHIP TO CHRIST. I AM DEPENDING ON CHRIST'S MIGHTY POWER THAT WORKS WITHIN ME.

LOVE,
SUGAR
MS. JUANITA WILSON++

There Is a Love That Can Not Be Broken

Even before he made the world, God loved us and chose us in Christ to be holy and without fault in his eyes. God decided in advance to adopt us into His own family by bringing us to Himself through Jesus Christ. This is what He wanted to do, and it gave Him great pleasure. So we praise God for the glorious grace He has poured out on us who belong to His dear Son. He is so rich in kindness and grace that He purchased our freedom with the blood of His Son and forgave our sins. He has shown His kindness to us, along with all the wisdom and understanding.

And this is the plan: At the right time, He will bring everything together under the authority of Christ—everything in the heavens and on earth because we are united with Christ. We have received an inheritance from God, for He chose us in advance, and He made everything work out according to His plan. And now you have also heard the truth—the good news that God saved you. And when you believe in Christ, He identifies you as His own by giving you the Holy Spirit, which He promised long ago.

I am asking God, the glorious Father of our Lord Jesus Christ, to give you spiritual wisdom and insight so that you might grow in your knowledge of God. I pray that your heart will be flooded with light so that you can understand the confidence and hope He has given to those He calls His holy people, who are His rich and glorious inheritance. I also pray that you will understand the incredible greatness of God's power for us who believe Him. This is the same mighty power that raised Christ from the dead and seated Him in the place of honor at God's right hand.

So now there is no condemnation for those who belong to Christ Jesus, and because you belong to Him, the power of the life-giving spirit has freed you from the power of sin that leads to death. His love cannot be broken.

Ms. Juanita Wilson-Sugar

This Is Real love

Do not believe everyone who claims to speak from the Spirit. You must test them to see if the Spirit they have comes from God. But there are many false prophets in the world. This is how we will know if they have the Spirit of God: If a person claims to be a prophet, acknowledging that Jesus Christ came in a real body, that person has the Spirit of God. But if someone claims to be a prophet and does not acknowledge the truth about Jesus, that person is not from God. Such a person has the spirit of the Antichrist, which you heard is coming into the world and indeed is already here. But you belong to God. You have already won a victory over those people because the Spirit Who lives in you is greater than the spirit who lives in the world. And those who know God listen to us. If they do not belong to God, they will not listen to us. That is how we know if someone has the Spirit of truth or the spirit of deception.

Let us continue to love one another, for love comes from God. Anyone who loves is a child of God and knows God. But anyone who does not love does not know God, for God is love. God showed how much He loves us by sending His one and only Son into the world so that we might have eternal life through Him. This is real love—not that we love God, but that He loved us and sent His Son as a sacrifice to take away our sins. Since God loved us that much, we surely ought to love each other. No one has ever seen God. But if we love each other, God lives in us, and His love is brought to full expression in us. And God has given us His Spirit as proof that we live in Him and He in us. Our God sent Jesus to be the Savior of the world.

Such love has no fear because perfect love expels all fear. If we are afraid, it is for fear of punishment, and this shows that we have

not fully experienced His perfect love. We love each other because
He loved us first. And He has given us this command: Those who
love God must also love their fellow believers.

LOVE, SUGAR
Ms. JUANITA WILSON

The Morning Light

John was called, and you, my little son, will be called the prophet of the Most High because you will prepare the way for the Lord. You will tell His people how to find salvation through the forgiveness of their sins.

He has sent us a mighty Savior from the royal line of His servant David, just as He promised through His holy prophets long ago. Now we can be saved from our enemies and from all who hate us. He has been merciful to our ancestors by remembering His sacred covenant. We have been rescued from our enemies, so we can serve God without fear, in holiness and righteousness, for as long as we live.

He shows mercy from generation to generation to all who fear Him. His mighty arm has done tremendous things! He has scattered the proud and haughty ones. He has brought down princes from their thrones and exalted the humble. He has filled the hungry with good things and sent the rich away with empty hands.

Because of God's tender mercy, the morning light from heaven is about to break upon us, to give light to those who sit in darkness and in the shadow of death, and to guide us to the path of peace. Our Lord Jesus is our morning light.

John grew up and became strong in spirit. And he lived in the wilderness until he began his public ministry in Israel. So what ministry has God given you?

Sis. Sugar
Ms. Juanita Wilson

An Everlasting Power and Love

Come to me with your ears wide open. Listen, and you will find life. Seek the Lord while you can find Him. Call on Him while He is near.

Let the wicked change their ways and banish the very thought of doing wrong. Let them turn to the Lord that He may have mercy on them.

"My thoughts are nothing like your thoughts," says the Lord. "And My ways are far beyond anything you could imagine. For just as the heavens are higher than the earth, so My ways are higher than your ways and My thoughts higher than your thoughts." If we could think like our God, this world would be so different. We would love each other the way that God does. We wouldn't be fighting all the time and hurting each other just because we can.

Wake up before it is too late. Are you going to miss the greatest love of your life just because you don't want to believe that He is real? Do you have any idea how much that hurts our God? Our God is always the same; He never changes. The same God Who loved you in your mother's womb is the same God Who died on the cross just for you. He came and died because He didn't want to live without you. No one could save you but Jesus. He was the only one Who could bring you back to the Father.

For I am not ashamed of the good news about Christ our Lord. It is the power of God at work, saving everyone who believes, the Jews and also the Gentiles. The good news tells us how God made us right in His sight. This is accomplished from start to finish by faith. As the Scriptures say,

"It is through faith that a righteous person has life." He has done everything to get you home so that you can be with Him forever. Don't miss the greatest gift of your life. These events will bring great honor to the Lord's name; they will be an everlasting sign of His power and love.

Love always,
Ms. Juanita Wilson

We Live to Live Again

I heard a pastor say something so wonderful about God's
children.
When we belong to God, we do not die. We only fall asleep,
and when our Lord Jesus
comes back for His children, we will live again.
Our destiny is to be with our Lord Jesus forever and ever.
Our life with our God is forever and ever. It is for eternity.
We live to love like Jesus,
To touch someone's life just like Jesus,
To tell someone about His grace and the love He has for
them,
To forgive like Jesus because He forgave us,
To care for all of God's children the way that He does.
"We live to live again,"
To be with our Lord forever and ever,
To love Him forever and ever,
To live the way that He did here on Earth.
He lived and lives again,
Our Lord went to sleep and He rose again,
Our God is alive and He is well.
If He made you in His image, our God knows the plans He has
for us.
They are plans for your good and not for disaster,
To give you a future and hope.

We live to live again,
Our God asks us to obey His word, and if you love our God,
you will live again.
Home is where I want to be.

Love,
Sugar
Ms. Juanita Wilson

My Beloved

Do you know how much our God loves you and me? He calls us His beloved. He is pouring His love out on us every day of our lives. We are of great value to our God. Do you know that He calls us precious? You are so important to our God. He loves you more than anything.

Our God gave His Son to die in our place. Now that we are in Christ, nothing can separate us from our God. I gave you a part of me to live in you forever. The Holy Spirit has always been with you. He goes where you go, He sees what you see, and He hears what you hear. He knows what is in your heart, good or bad. He is always with you. You cannot hide from our God.

Our God put Jesus in you, and then He put you in Jesus so that He could love you the same way He loves His Son. And because of the love that He has for you, you are the beloved of all time. The life that you have, God put into you, and your life belongs to our God. Special is who you are to our God. He died on the cross for your sins. Thank you, my Lord.

Our challenge and mission, if we choose to accept them, are to be like Jesus at all times. We have the Father, the Son, and Holy Spirit to help us win. Your life can change if you know how to be wonderfully loved. When God looks at you, He sees nothing wrong. All He sees is Jesus. I have something to give you. I'm going to teach you to trust in

Me. Beloved, you are the love of My life, and nothing can take you out of My hands. I will always love you. You are My beloved.

Always and forever,
Sis. Sugar
Ms. Juanita Wilson

Love Is Always Here

Love is always here. It never goes away. Love is that close. If you need Him, He is always there. Love never stops. His love took my place. His love is to die just for me. His love will never leave me or forsake me. His love has always been here with me. His love leads me down the right path. His love goes before me. His love covers my back. His love woke me up this morning. His love goes wherever I go. His love provides for me. His love redeems me. His love saves me from death. The love that has always been with me. The love who made me in His image. The love that is here right now. His love that is always here. Love is the one Who wants to do life with me right now. Love has always been waiting for you.

The Lord is good to everyone. He showers compassion on all His creation. All of your works will thank You, Lord, and Your faithful followers will praise You. They will speak of the glory of Your Kingdom; they will give examples of Your power. They will tell about Your mighty deeds and about the majestic glory of Your reign. For Your kingdom is an everlasting kingdom. You rule throughout all generations.

The Lord always keeps His promises; He is gracious in all that He does. The Lord helps the fallen and lifts those bent beneath their loads. The eyes of all look to You in hope; You give them their food as they need it. When You open Your hand, You satisfy the hunger and thirst of every living thing. The Lord is righteous in everything that He does; He is filled with kindness. The Lord is close to all who call on Him—yes, to all who call on Him in truth. He grants the desires of those who fear Him. He hears their cries for help and rescues them. The law protects all those who love Him, but He destroys the wicked. I will praise the Lord, and may everyone on earth bless His holy name forever and ever.

Love is in place,
Sis. Sugar / Ms. Juanita Wilson

God Has Given His Promise and His Oath

So let us stop going over the basic teachings about Christ again and again. Let us go on instead and become mature and understanding. Surely, we don't need to start again with the fundamental importance of repenting from evil deeds and placing our faith in God.

For it is impossible to bring back to repentance those who were once enlightened—those who have experienced the good things of heaven and shared in the Holy Spirit, who have tasted the goodness of the Word of God and the power of the age to come—and who then turn away from God. It is impossible to bring such people back to repentance; by rejecting the Son of God, they themselves are nailing Him to the cross once again and holding Him up to public shame.

For God is not unjust. He will not forget how hard you have worked for Him and how you have shown your love to Him by caring for other believers, as you still do. Our greatest desire is that you will keep on loving others as long as life lasts in order to make certain that what you hope for will come true. Then you will not become spiritually dull and indifferent. Instead, you will follow the example of those who are going to inherit God's promises because of their faith and their endurance. There was no one greater to swear by. God took an oath in His own name, saying, "I will certainly bless you, and I will multiply your descendants beyond numbers." So we wait patiently for what God has promised to us.

So God has given both His promise and His own; these two things are unchanged because it is impossible for God to lie. Therefore, we who have fled to Him for refuge can have great confidence as we hold on to the hope that lies before us. This hope is strong and trustworthy for ourselves; it leads us through the curtains into God's sanctuary. Jesus has already gone in there for us; He has become our Eternal High Priest.

Ms. Juanita Wilson
Sister Sugar

Because of the Jesus
Who Lives in Me

TODAY, SOMETHING WONDERFUL HAPPENED TO ME.

TODAY, SOMEONE SAID SOMETHING SO BEAUTIFUL THAT IT MADE ME CRY.

HE SAID, "BECAUSE OF THE JESUS WHO LIVES IN YOU, YOU ARE A BEAUTIFUL WOMAN."

TO HEAR WHAT PEOPLE SEE WHEN THEY LOOK AT ME IS SO AMAZING TO ME.

TO SEE THE LOVE I HAVE FOR HIM BECAUSE HE IS IN LOVE WITH ME.

TO SEE THE KINDNESS THAT HE HAS PUT IN ME.

TO SEE THE JOY THAT HE HAS PLACED IN ME.

TO SEE HIS CHILDREN THE WAY HE DOES.

IT IS BECAUSE OF THE JESUS WHO LIVES INSIDE OF ME.

HE IS THE ONE WHO GAVE ME HIS PEACE THAT THE WORLD COULD NOT GIVE.

IT MAKES ME HAPPY WHEN I THINK ABOUT WHO LOVES ME.

WHO DIED FOR ME? WHO FIGHTS FOR ME? WHO HAS KEPT ME ALL THESE YEARS?

WHO WAS THERE IN THE BEGINNING? JESUS WAS.

IT IS SO GOOD TO KNOW THAT YOU HAVE ALWAYS BEEN HERE WITH ME, MY LORD. THANK YOU, HOLY SPIRIT, FOR BEING SO CLOSE.

BECAUSE OF THE JESUS WHO LIVES IN ME, I AM A BEAUTIFUL WOMAN.

Love always,
Sis. Sugar
Ms. Juanita Wilson

See Your Life through God's Eyes

First things first. You and I are children of the Most High God. We were created in His mind before we were ever born. He knew me before I was in my mother's womb. He created me in His image. Before the foundation of the world was formed.

O Lord, you have examined my heart and know everything about me. You know when I sit down or stand up. You know my thoughts, even when I'm far away. You see me when I travel and when I rest at home. You know everything I do. You know what I am going to say even before I say it, Lord. You go before me and follow me. You place Your hand of blessings on my head. Such knowledge is too wonderful for me, too great for me to understand! You are so close to me, my Lord.

You made all the delicate inner parts of my body and knit me together in my mother's womb. You watched me as I was being formed in utter seclusion, as I was woven together in the darkness of the womb. You saw me before I was born.

Every day of my life was recorded in Your book, Lord. Every moment was laid out before a single day had passed. How precious are Your thoughts about me, O God. And when I wake up, You are still with me. We were created to be God's family forever and ever. Our God has always been in place because of Who He is. He has not changed His mind about you and me. We are His family, and we will always be.

HE IS THE SAME GOD AS YESTERDAY, TODAY, AND FOREVER. WHEN GOD LOOKS AT YOU AND ME, ALL HE SEES ARE HIS HOLY CHILDREN BECAUSE OF THE BLOOD OF HIS SON, JESUS CHRIST. HE MADE YOU AND I PERFECT JUST FOR HIM. SPECIAL IS WHO YOU ARE TO OUR GOD. HE HOPES THAT YOU AND I WILL ACCEPT THE GIFT OF LOVE THAT HIS SON HAS GIVEN TO YOU AND ME.

SEARCH ME, O GOD, AND KNOW MY HEART. TEST ME AND KNOW MY ANXIOUS THOUGHTS. POINT OUT ANYTHING IN ME THAT OFFENDS YOU, AND LEAD ME ALONG THE PATH OF EVERLASTING LIFE. AMEN.

LOVE, SUGAR
MS. JUANITA WILSON

HE HOPES THAT WE WILL ACCEPT THE GIFT OF LOVE THAT HIS SON HAS GIVEN TO YOU AND ME. SO THAT WE CAN LIVE THE LIFE THAT HE HAS PREPARED FOR YOU AND FOR ME. YOU HAVE TO SEE WHO GOD SEES WHEN HE LOOKS AT YOU. WE ARE GOD'S HOLY CHILDREN. WE ARE CHILDREN OF THE LIVING GOD. SEE YOURSELF THROUGH GOD'S EYES.

You Forgave

Do you ever think about the things that God has done for you? How good is He to you? Listen carefully to what God the Lord is saying, for He speaks peace to His faithful people. But let them not return to their foolish ways. Surely His salvation is near to those who fear Him, so our land will be filled with His glory.

Lord, you forgave the guilt of your people. Yes, You covered all their sins. Did you hear what that said? He can forgive us. Wow, that is so amazing to know that our God can forgive us. All we have to do is ask Him. And ask Him to help us not to do it again. There is a love that our God has for you and me that is so amazing if you could just believe that He is real.

Our God held back His fury. Now restore us again, O God of our salvation. Put aside your anger against us once more. Won't You revive us again, so Your people can rejoice in You, Lord? Show us Your unfailing love, O Lord, and grant us Your salvation.

His unfailing love and truth have met together. His righteousness and peace have kissed! Truth springs up from the earth, and righteousness smiles down from heaven. Yes, the Lord pours down His blessings. Righteousness goes before Him, preparing the way for His steps. Our God has forgiven you. Now you need to forgive yourself.

Sister Sugar
Ms. Juanita Wilson

Unto Us

For a child is born to us. A son given to us. The government will rest on his shoulders. And he will be called Wonderful Counselor, Mighty God, Everlasting Father, Prince of Peace.

Unto to us, He came from heaven. He left His throne to be born like you and me. He came to see what it was like to be like you and me. How it is to be human.

To be sad like you. To be hurt like you. To be lied to just like you.

To be mistreated like you and still be God. He was tempted like you, and He did no wrong.

He was nailed to the cross for our sins. And to be raised from the dead, and to be alive again. Our God, Whose name is Jesus. "Our Savior." He came to see what it's like to be you and me. Because He is our God.

Thank You, my Lord, for the love that You have for Your people. You and I are children of the Most High God. Thank You, my Lord, for giving up everything just to save me.

Sugar always,
Ms. Juanita Wilson

Our God's Grace

Because of God's grace, you and I have been saved. We are able to go to heaven to be with Jesus.

Because He loved us so much, He left heaven to come and save you and me.

There is not one person who has the right to live because of our sins. But our God knows the beginning, and he knows the end. And He is praying for you and for me. That we will accept the gift of love that Jesus gave for you and for me.

God wants you and me to live like Adam and Eve before they sinned. To have God's peace. God's happiness. God's joy and God's love. That's His unconditional love for you and for me.

Our God's grace.

Is that we can live the way that Adam and Eve were supposed to before they sinned? Not having to worry because our God has us in the palm of His hand. And all that He asks of you and me is to love Him and to trust in Him and His Word. To believe that He is your God. The Almighty, Who lives in heaven. And that we would put our hopes and our dreams in His hands because God can do anything. Nothing is impossible for our God. Our Father, our Jesus. And I call Him my daddy because He loves us so much, and He wants us to have a wonderful life right here on earth. And all He asks of you and me is to obey His Word.

I love You, Jesus
Ms. Juanita Wilson
Sugar

Please Forgive Me

Have you ever asked our God for forgiveness? But you can't forgive anyone else? Do you know that if you can't forgive, God can't forgive you? For you to forgive is not for them. It is for you. We have all made mistakes. We make them all the time because we are not perfect. There is only one perfect one, and His name is Jesus Christ, our Lord. Do you know what Lord means? One having power and authority over others, a ruler to whom service and obedience are due: God, Christ.

I have made a lot of mistakes in my life. Some I didn't remember, and God reminded me so that I could ask for forgiveness. Sometimes we do things without thinking about them, and we wish that we hadn't done them. But thank God, we can ask our God for forgiveness, and He will if we mean it from our hearts. Our God goes by what is in our hearts, not just what we say. Now I live in peace and not under condemnation. Thank You, my Lord, for dying on the cross for my sins.

Do you know that you can be free if you want to be? Christ, our Savior, has done everything that needed to be done to save you and me. Do you even want to be saved? All you have to do is say yes to our God. God bless you. And thank You, Lord, for Your forgiveness. In Psalm 145:19, "He grants the desires of those who fear him; he hears their cries for help and rescues them." God will forgive you if you ask. He is in love with you. Hallelujah!

Love always,
Sugar
Ms. Juanita Wilson

You Must Pay Attention

Love pays attention. I am talking about our God. He is the one Who pays attention to everything in our lives. He is the one Who created your heart so that you could love like him. He is the one Who created your mind so that you could think like him.

The one Who chose the color of your eyes and the color of your skin. He thought about everything when He created you and me. You are important to our God.

You are the one who brings life into this world. You are the one who was chosen by our God. You were chosen to be a mother, a sister, an aunt, a wife, and someone's best friend. It doesn't matter who they are; you just have to love them, even if it's from a distance, and keep on praying. When we learn to love like our God, we begin to pay attention to God's children the way that He does. We have to pay attention the same way He pays attention to us.

We have to see God's children the way that He does, with compassion, love, mercy, and peace at all times with each other. We must pay attention to the homeless, the sick, the misused, and the mistreated.

For the Bible says, "If you were blind, you wouldn't be guilty." Jesus replied, "But you remain guilty because you claim you can see." We must pay attention to what we see because of our God. Open up your eyes and see.

Sister Sugar
Ms. Juanita Wilson

A Man of Complete Integrity

Men of Integrity, how blessed we are to have you
You have been the Priest of the Home
Honoring God with your walk just for Him
Teaching your children the right way to go
To Trust in their God Who loves them so much
And because of that Love He has for them
He will always be Faithful to them
Men of Integrity—you are Faithful, Loving, Kind, and Honest
You have Compassion, Patience
The same character as our God
Protecting your Family, Providing for your Family
Being there when they need you, Never turning your back on them
Even when you know they have to learn it the hard way sometimes
But you are still there to pick up the pieces of their life
Men of Integrity—you never give up on your family
Just like our God never gave up on you learning from your mistakes
And asking Him to help you not do it again
Men of Integrity—God declared you Righteous, and you wear it well
Your God Who preserved your life and made
you innocent because of His Blood
He has brought you into His presence forever and ever Amen—Amen
Men of Integrity—Always Stand Up for Your God

Always and forever,
Love, Sis. Sugar

Am I Not Worthy of Your Praise?

I have loved you before the beginning of time. I have not stopped loving you. You are my children, and you will always be.

You act like I stopped loving you. When did I do that? What day was it? What time was it? I don't remember when I stopped loving you.

I am always the same. I never change.

I am the same as yesterday, today, tomorrow, and forever. That is Who I am.

You don't love Me anymore. You don't praise Me in your home anymore.

You don't read your Word anymore. You have forgotten who I am.

I have never let you down. I have never failed you.

You don't talk to Me anymore. I only hear from you when something goes wrong. Do you even think about Me? I am always here with you.

I miss your singing and dancing for Me. I miss you talking to Me and listening to what I have to say. You stopped praying to Me. So what is wrong?

I have not stopped loving you. Why have you stopped loving Me?

I gave up everything so you would know how much I love you.

I gave My Son to save you. Am I not worthy of your praise?

My love will endure forever and ever.

That will never change. It will always be.

If only you understood that Christ will make His home in your heart as you trust in Him. Your roots will grow into God's love and keep you strong. And may you have the power to understand, as all God's people should, how wide, how long, how high, and how deep His love is. Now all glory to God, Who is able, through His mighty power at work within us, to accomplish infinitely more than we might ask or think.

Am I not worthy of your praise?

Juanita Wilson
Sister Sugar

You Already Have It

So now there is no condemnation for those who belong to Christ Jesus. And because you belong to Him, the power of the life-giving Spirit has freed you from the power of sin, which leads to death.

My prayer is not for the world but for those You have given Me, because they belong to You. All who are Mine belong to You, and You have given them to Me, so they bring Me glory. Now I am departing from this world; they are staying in this world, but I am coming to You, Holy Father. You have given Me Your name. Now protect them by the power of Your name so that they will be united just as We are. During My time here, I protected them by the power of Your name You gave me. I guarded them so that not one was lost, except the one headed for destruction, as the Scriptures foretold. I'm not asking You to take them out of the world but to keep them safe from the evil one. They do not belong to this world any more than I do.

Just as you sent Me into the world, I am sending them into the world. And I give Myself as a holy sacrifice for them, so they can be made holy by Your truth. I am praying not only for these disciples but also for all who will ever believe in Me through their message.

I pray that they all will be one, just as You and I are one—as You are in Me, Father, and I am in You. And may they be in Us so that the world will believe You sent Me.

Father, the world doesn't know You, but I do. And these disciples know that You sent Me. I have revealed You to them,

AND I WILL CONTINUE TO DO SO. THEN YOUR LOVE FOR ME WILL BE IN THEM, AND I WILL BE IN THEM.

FATHER, I WANT THESE WHOM YOU HAVE GIVEN TO ME TO BE WITH ME WHERE I AM. I WANT YOU TO BE WITH ME IN HEAVEN FOR ETERNITY.

I LOVE YOU, LORD.
SIS. SUGAR
MS. JUANITA WILSON

Let Us Do Something New

For I am about to do something new.
See, I have already begun! Do you not see it?
I will make a pathway through the wilderness.
I will create rivers in the dry wasteland.
Let us do something new just for our God.
To love someone who we don't even know.
To be kind to everyone like Jesus, our Lord.
To feed someone who is hungry just because.
To clothe someone who has nothing.
To give someone something to drink because they are thirsty.
To love God's people each and every day the way He loves us.
You and I are here to do something new just for our Lord
    and Savior.
So let us make Him proud that we are His children and that
    we love Him too.
You and I are children of God, Who lives in Heaven.
I love You, my Lord, because You have been so good to me.
And I want to thank You for being my Father.

Love, Your daughter
Ms. Juanita Wilson
Sister Sugar

To Kiss Our King

Our entire being is fashioned as an instrument of praise. The first is the concept of prostrating oneself before God—lying flat on one's face before the Lord. The word *worship* means "to adore." Worship entails adoration—to adore, worship, to be extremely fond of—adorer. Adoration—"the act of adoring, state of being adored." When we love and worship our God, we are adoring Him, loving Him deeply and respectfully.

The word simply means to blow a kiss to our God. I plead with you to give your bodies to God because of all He has done for you. Let them be a living and holy sacrifice—the kind He will find acceptable. This is truly the way to worship Him. Let God transform you into a new person by changing the way that you think. Then you will learn to know God's will for you, which is good, pleasing, and perfect. I give each of you this warning: Don't think you are better than you really are. Be honest in your evaluation of yourselves, measuring yourselves by the faith God has given you.

To kiss our King is to fall in love with Jesus. To honor Him for Who He really is. To live a good life is to kiss our King. To forgive others is to kiss our King. To feed our enemies is to kiss our King. To love someone who doesn't love you is to kiss our King.

All the good things in our lives come from heaven. In His grace, God has given us different gifts for doing certain things well. So if God has given you the ability to prophesy, speak out with as much faith as God has given you. If the gift is serving others, serve them well. If you are a teacher, teach well. If your gift is to encourage others, be encouraging. If it is giving, give generously. If God has given you leadership ability, take responsibility seriously. And if your gift is showing kindness to others, do it gladly. Don't just pretend to love others. Really love them. Love each other with genuine affection and take delight in honoring each other. Don't let evil conquer you, but conquer evil by doing good. Do things in such a way that everyone can see that you are honorable. Do all that you can to live in peace with all of God's children.

Love,
Your daughter
Sis. Sugar / Ms. Juanita Wilson

All You Have to Do Is Reach for Him

Close your eyes and imagine Jesus standing on a mountain with His disciples. You and others were standing at the bottom of the mountain, and you were there because you needed healing from Jesus. But you are all the way in the back. Not close enough to touch Him but believing that if you could, you would be healed by His grace and love for you. Even if you are in the back, His love for you, no matter where you are, can touch you. His love is so great that nothing can stop it. It has always been there, and it always will be. Jesus's love has been there from the beginning, and it will be there 'till the end. He has that kind of love that never stops. His love endures forever and ever reach for Him, reach for him. He has always been in place for you and for me. Trust your God with everything you own and know that He only wants the best for you and me. All you have to do is reach for Him. He is already there.

Love, Sugar
Ms. Juanita Wilson

There Is a Man in the House

There Is A Man In The House
Who Takes Care Of All My Needs
There Is A Man In The House
Who Is Always Doing Something Just For Me
There Is A Man In The House
Who I Can Talk To At Any Time
There Is A Man In This House
Who Is Always Blessing Me
There Is A Man In The House
Who Loves Me
There Is A Man In The House
Who's Always With Me
There Is A Man In The House
Who Protects Me
There Is A Man In The House
Who Saved Me
There Is A Man In The House
Who Died On The Cross Just For Me
There Is A Man In The House
And His Name Is Jesus

Love, Your daughter
Sugar
Ms. Juanita Wilson

Last Night, Jesus Woke Me Up

Last night, Jesus woke me
up out of a deep sleep.
The thunder was so loud
that it scared me,
and I could not go back to sleep.

A member of my family told me
that a dog that lived next door
to her, in Corpus Christi
was awakened by the thunder
and barked for the rest of the night.

Even the dog knew who God is.
The thunder scared him so
badly that he didn't stop barking
until daylight.

Even a dog knew how
powerful our God is,
so why don't we?

No one can make it thunder.
No one can make it lightning.
No one can make it rain.
No one can make the sun shine
No one can make the air that we breathe.
No one but our Lord.

Thank You, Lord
for reminding us
of who we are

The Almighty God,
Father,
Jesus,
Our daddy,
don't forget His Holy Spirit,
Thank You! Jesus.

Love always,
Sugar

I Have Chosen This Temple

In the time of old, the Lord's Spirit was in the temple. The building was the temple. But now the temple is you and me because of the Lord's Spirit. The Holy Spirit lives in you and me.

If you faithfully follow me as David your father did, obeying all of my commands, decrees, and regulations, then I will establish the throne of your dynasty. You need to understand that God is your dynasty. He is the one Who controls everything. Your life was planned before you were ever born. God knew you before the beginning of time. He has always known you. He knows what you are thinking. He knows what you are about to do next. He knows everything about you, good or bad. You cannot hide anything from our God.

Jesus could only be at one place at one time, and the Holy Spirit can be everywhere at the same time. He can individually help and guide each one of us at the same time. For the Father Who knows all hearts knows what the Spirit is saying, and the Spirit pleads for us, believers, in harmony with God's will. And we know that God causes everything to work together for the good of those who love Him and are called according to His purpose for them. For God knew His people in advance, and He chose them to become like His Son so that His Son would be the firstborn among many brothers and sisters. And having called them, He gave them right standing with Himself. He gave them His glory. And all who are led by His Spirit are children of the living God.

thank You for loving me,
Ms. Juanita Wilson

Thank You for Bringing Me Back

Lord, thank You for bringing me back each time that I have died.

Because if You had not, I would have missed heaven. Because of my lifestyle and doing what I wanted to do, it was going to cost me my life in heaven with You. Because I thought I could do what I wanted to do. That is not the truth.

I thank You for loving me so much that You kept me in Your arms and brought me back to life again so that I could have another chance to get to know You and to get it right with You, my Lord. Thank You, Jesus. Thank You, Jesus, for seeing what I didn't see in myself. Thank You for being with me before the beginning of time. And because of the love that You have for me, I can tell the whole world how good You are to me. Thank You, my Lord. You are a wonderful Father to us all.

You know that the devil has been trying to kill me all of my life, but because of You, my Lord, I am still here. I have Jesus, and Jesus has me. Because of the plan that You have for my future, I just want to thank You, my Lord. You have been watching over me all the days of my life. Thank You for being my King now and forever.

Love always,
Sister Sugar
Ms. Juanita Wilson

My Perfect Father

The Lord is their fortress of salvation to His anointed. Save Your people and bless Your inheritance. Be their shepherd also, and carry them forever. I pray to You, Oh Lord, my rock. Do not turn a deaf ear to me. For if You are silent, I might as well give up and die, Lord.

Praise the Lord! He has heard my cry for mercy. The Lord is my strength and my shield. I trust Him with all my heart. He helps me, and my heart is filled with joy. I burst out in songs of thanksgiving. Bless Your special possession, Lord.

Though a mighty army surrounds me, my heart will not be afraid. Even if I am attacked, I will remain confident. The one thing I ask of the Lord—the thing I seek the most—is to live in the house of the Lord all the days of my life. I will contemplate His beauty, and I will study at His feet. God holds my head and shoulders above all who try to pull me down. I'm headed for His place to offer anthems that will raise the roof. Already I'm singing God's song; I'm making music to my God.

You've always been right there for me. Don't turn Your back on me now. Don't throw me out. Don't abandon me. You've always kept the door open. My father and mother walked out and left me, but God took me in. Point me down Your highway, God; direct me along a well-lighted street; show my enemies whose side you're on.

I'm sure now. I'll see God's goodness on earth. Stay with God! Take heart. Don't quit. I'll say it again: Stay with God.

Love,
Sugar
Ms. Juanita Wilson

A Brief Moment

"For a brief moment, I abandoned you, but with great compassion, I will take you back. In a burst of anger, I turned My face away for a little while. But with everlasting love, I will have compassion on you," says the Lord, your Redeemer.

Because of My faithful love for you, My faithful love will remain forever and ever. For eternity. Don't worry about the wicked or envy those who do wrong. Trust in the Lord and do good. Then you will live safely in the land and prosper. Take delight in the Lord, and He will give you your heart's desires. Commit everything you do to the Lord. Trust Him, and He will help you.

Stop being angry! Turn away from your rage! Do not lose your temper. It only leads to harm. It is better to be godly and have little than to be evil and rich. For the strength of the wicked will be shattered, but the Lord takes care of the godly. Day by day, the Lord takes care of the innocent, and they will receive an inheritance that lasts forever. They will not be disgraced in hard times; even in famine, they will have more than enough.

The Lord directs the steps of the godly. He delights in every detail of our lives. Though they stumble, they will never fall, for the Lord holds them by the hand. He will keep them safe forever, but the children of the wicked will die. Make God's laws your own so that you will never stray from His path.

Our God saved us, and we can find shelter in His arms. "My covenant of blessing will never be broken," says the

Lord, Who has mercy on you. These benefits are enjoyed by
the servants of the Lord; their vindication will come from
me. "I, the Lord, have spoken!"

Thank You, my Lord,
Sis. Sugar
Ms. Juanita Wilson

I Come to You, Lord, Because You Have My Destiny

Dear Father,

I come to You because of my destiny. I come because You know everything.

I come because You have a plan for my life, and help me step into my destiny.

Lord, because You know everything, You placed a child into the Nile River so that he would be found by a princess,

To be taken care of by someone with power over

His people, and that he would be that child who would help to set them free.

This was Your plan; from the day he was born, he had a destiny. God had already planned what he was going to do.

In Exodus 2 and 3, God told Moses that he would tell Pharaoh to "Let my people go."

The plan God has for us, we don't always know, but God does, and if we just have faith in Him, everything is for the good of our God's kingdom. Trust in our God.

Have faith.

Know that He does have a plan for each and every one of His children.

Stop being afraid of your future; our God has a plan for you. You cannot fail; our God will put you where you need to be.

Jesus loves you,
Juanita Wilson
"Sugar"

God Deepest Secret

You and I are God's deepest secrets. We were born for a purpose—to change God's children's minds about Him.

Do you know that this is not our home? Your home is in heaven with Jesus. The wisdom that God gives you and me is through His Spirit. No one else can give it to you but our God. The power comes from Him, even when we were in our mother's womb.

The Lord says in Psalm 51:6, "But you desire honesty from the womb; teaching me wisdom even there. Our God will always lead you to the right path because he is our God."

In 1 Corinthians 1:30, "God has united you with Christ Jesus. For our benefit God made him to be wisdom itself." Christ made us right with God; He made us pure and holy, and He freed us from sin.

If you do not believe in God, 1 Corinthians 2:9 says, "No eye has seen, no ear has heard and no mind has imagined what God has prepared for those who love him."

God's deepest secret is you and me.

Love always,
Sis. Sugar
Ms. Juanita Wilson

Women of God

You have to know who you are to our God. God's gifts (you and I) put men's best dreams to shame. We were created to bring life into this world, the next generations. Our children, their children, and our great-grandchildren are a part of you and me.

Difficult tasks are going to come your way in this life. Now how you go through it is left up to you. The ones that you would rather not do, that will take the most effort, cause the most pain, and may be the greatest struggle. Bring a blessing with it when it comes.

We all have to learn how to endure because it makes us strong. If you never have trials, how can you know how strong you really are? Sometimes we have to be knocked down just so we can get back up again. Our God knew that we were going to have to be strong in order to be able to make it through this life.

Where is the respect that we used to have for ourselves? Where is the respect that we had for each other as women of God? What happened to the respect that we had for our God when we didn't want to disappoint Him anymore? He has called us to be His children. We are the children of His light.

Don't turn away from My instructions. Take My word to heart. Follow My commands, and you will live. Don't turn your back on wisdom, for she will protect you. Love her, and she will guard you. If you prize wisdom, she will make you great. Embrace her, and she will honor you. Guard them, for they are the key to life.

Listen carefully to My words, for they bring life to those who find them and healing to their whole body. Guard your heart above all else, for it determines the course of your life. For fear of the Lord is the foundation of wisdom, and if you become wise, you will be the one to benefit. We are the mothers of this world.

Love always,
Sugar
Ms. Juanita Wilson

In His Rest

The Bible tells us about God's rest. It tells us that Jesus, the Son of God, Who is the High Priest, has gone to heaven Himself to help us. So therefore, let us never stop trusting in Him. It tells about our God, Who rested on the seventh day. It says that God's promise still stands for you and me today.

Today is a day when, if you hear Him call, don't harden your hearts against God. Our God, Who lives in heaven, has put His rest in place for you and me. His promise has not changed. He is the same as yesterday, today, and forever.

Our God, Who no one can stop what He has prepared for you and me. I thank You, my God, for putting everything in place for Your children, even right now and forever. To know that I have a God Who cannot die, oh my God. The God of heaven's army. The Great I Am. The Prince of Peace. The Lord of lords. His name is Jesus Christ, the Son of the Living God. His rest still stands for you and me. Everything is already in place. That is how much He loves you and me. Praise the Lord! Hallelujah to His name.

Love,
Sugar
Ms. Juanita Wilson

Standing in the Shadow of God

When you're standing in the shadow of God, you are under His protection. He is with you right here, right now. He will always be with you forever. Do you know that when you are in the shadow of God's love, even when you are sick, God's healing is always with you? If only you would believe. Do you know how much God loves you? He loves you more than anything in this world. You are under God's shadow. You need to know that everything is going to be alright. There is nothing that our God can't do. You are in the shadow of God. You are behind Jesus Christ, our Lord.

He will always go before you. He will protect you in times of trouble. He will never leave you or forsake you because you belong to Him. He will never leave you, no matter what happens. Our God is in love with you. He came and died on the cross just to set you free. Even when you're not sure of Him, He has always been sure about you. We are God's family. He calls us His beloved children. We are God's holy children. That is how much He cares about you and me. Now remember that you are standing in the shadow of God, and you are standing behind the shadow of miracles. You have to know that God is the Almighty God. He can do what He wants to do whatever He wants to do. No one can stop our God.

Come to Me, My children. "Come to me, all of you who are weary and carry heavy burdens, and I will give you rest. Take my yoke upon you. Let me teach you, because I am humble and gentle at heart, and you will find rest for your souls. For my yoke is easy to bear, and the burden I give you is light." Thank You, my Lord, for loving us so much that You didn't want to live without us. Thank You for Your life. Thank You for your life that You gave up just for me. How blessed we are.

You made me special,
Sister Sugar
Ms. Juanita Wilson

When I Cry

When I cry, I cry because I am happy
When I cry, I cry because He brought me through.
When I cry, I remember being hurt by someone,
Who said that he loves me.

When I cry, I cry because I make it through.
When I cry, I remember my children and
Where they are today, and I thank You, Lord.
When I cry, I remember being dead
More than once, and I'm still here.
Thank You, Lord.

When you see me cry, be happy for me.
Because there is someone out there
Who cannot cry.
When you see me cry, I'm crying
Because Jesus loves me so much.
When you see me cry,
These are tears of joy, love, peace, and happiness
That Jesus gave me.
So when you see me cry. Just be happy for me.
I got Jesus, and Jesus got me.

Love always,
Sugar
Juanita Wilson

Jesus, You Made Me Special

Do you know how special you are to Him? He is in love with you. He loves you more than anything in this world.

He knew that no one could save you but Him. He came on purpose, just for you. His love is the same as yesterday, today, and forever. His love is forever because of Who He is. Our God Himself is love, and He cannot die. He lives forever.

He thought about us before we were even born. Our lives were written in His book before a single day had passed. He was here from the beginning, and He will always be here with me.

Jesus was the first of the harvest. He is God's Son. He is our big brother. He is our Savior. He is our everything. You don't need anyone but Him. He is so close that He was with me in my mother's womb. He saw me before I was born.

He was there when I was born dead. He was there when I died twice, bringing Tina into this world. He saved Tina and me. He was there when I had my first heart attack and died. He was there when I had my second heart attack and didn't even know it. He was there with me when I had open-heart surgery and died on the table, and I am still here. Because of all He has done for me, I am so grateful that He has always been so close to me. He said He would never leave me or forsake me, and He never has. I have seen God breathe back into me, and I am grateful and thankful for the love that He has for me. I feel special because of what He has done just for me.

Special is who I am. Special because of Your blood. Special is here with me all the time. Jesus is the special one; He is our God. May God's peace always be with you.

I love You, Lord.
Ms. Juanita Wilson

The Purpose of Your Life

We were created for Him to love. He knew me before I was born. He saw me in my mother's womb. You made all the delicate inner parts of my body. You are that close to me, my Lord. You created me to love You, to honor You, to praise and worship You, my Lord.

You created me so that I could have a personal relationship with You, my Lord. You are the one Who I can talk to at any time. You are the one to Whom I can cry at any time. You are the one Who goes before me and follows me. You place your hand of blessing on my head. Thank You, my Lord.

Lord, You were there with me when I was born dead, and you are the one Who breathed life into me. The purpose of my life is to live a good life because of You, my Lord. You came on purpose to bring us back to our God. No one else could do it but You, my Lord.

I am to love You first because of Who You are. You are my Savior. You are my King. You are my Lord. You gave up Your life just for me. You are the one Who brought me back to my Father Who lives in heaven, the one Who sits high above everyone else, the one Who is watching you and me, just to see if you love Him enough to do it right just for Him.

This life is not about you and me; it is about our God. Do you love Him enough not to hurt Him anymore? You cannot hide from our God; He is everywhere.

Your life belongs to Jesus Christ, our Lord. You are not here to live your life the way that you want to. You are here to love like Jesus, to treat His children the same way that He did with love, to help whomever you can, to feed someone who is hungry, giving someone something to drink because they are thirsty. For you to do something for someone else because of Jesus. He is not just a God Who saved you, but a God Who cannot fail.

Love,
Sugar
Ms. Juanita Wilson

Thank You for Saving Me

You are the one Who saved me. I owe You my life, Lord. I could not have made it here if it were not for You. You delivered me from my sins, my Lord. You rescued me from danger and harm, and I thank You, my Lord. You preserve and guard me from injury. You saved me from my destruction and from being so lost.

You are my Savior. I am obligated to You for saving my life. Lord, I thank You for your everlasting love that You have for me. You have been with me all of my life. Thank You, Lord, for being so close. To know that You are always here is so amazing to me.

Thank You, Jesus, for making me right with my God. When He looks at me, He sees You, my Lord. To know that I am special to You means so much to me. To know that You will always love me, that is the greatest feeling of all. That You are in love with me. There is something so wonderful just knowing that You will always be with me.

I am not alone. In Psalm 145:18, "The Lord is close to all who call on him, yes, to all who call on him in truth." You can be truthful with our God. He knows everything. You can talk to our God at any time. He is always there with you. Thank You, my Lord, for Your precious love. Thank You for saving me. I love You, my Lord.

Love always,
Sugar
Ms. Juanita Wilson

When I Die

Just think that when I die, I don't have to be alone because Jesus is going to be there with me. To know that no matter what comes, Jesus is going to be with me.

Just think, when I leave here, I am going to be with my Lord in heaven, and that is so wonderful to know.

You know when I died this last time, I saw myself lying on the table in the emergency room. But my spirit was hovering at the top of the room. And my nephew came to the door and asked if he can say a prayer for me. And they told him it was too late. But he wouldn't leave, so they let him say his special prayer for me. And you know the rest of the story.

Just think, even in death, Jesus was with me. And I want to thank You, Lord, for not giving up on me because You reminded me that if You had not brought me back this last time, I wouldn't have made it to heaven to be with You. Thank You, my Lord.

So when I die, I don't have to be afraid because Jesus will be with me. And then I will be in heaven with Him forever and ever and ever.

Love, I thank You
Ms. Juanita Wilson

Be Careful

Imitate God, therefore, in everything you do, because you are His dear children. Live a life filled with love, following the example of Christ. He loved us and offered Himself as a sacrifice for us. Instead, let there be thankfulness to God. Don't be fooled by those who try to excuse their sins, for the anger of God will fall on all who disobey Him. Don't participate in the things these people do. For once, you were full of darkness, but now you have light from the Lord.

Carefully determine what pleases the Lord. For the light makes everything visible. This is why it is said, "Awake, O sleeper, rise up from the dead, and Christ will give you light." So be careful how you live. Don't live like fools, but like those who are wise. Make the most of every opportunity in these evil days.

Don't act thoughtlessly, but understand what the Lord wants you to do. Instead, be filled with the Holy Spirit—singing psalms, hymns, and spiritual songs among yourselves, making music to the Lord in your hearts, and giving thanks for everything to God the Father in the name of our Lord Jesus Christ. He is the Savior of His body, the church.

He gave up His life for her (you and me) to make her holy and clean, washed by the cleansing of God's Word. He did this to present her (you and me) to Himself as a glorious church without a spot, wrinkle, or any other blemish. Instead, she (you and me) will be holy and without fault. No one hates their own body but feeds and cares for it, just as Christ cares for the church. And we are members of the body.

We, too, are united as one with Christ. Be careful how you live because it is important to our God.

Be careful,
Sister Sugar
Ms. Juanita Wilson

You Can Unlock Your Own Door

For God, I Live; And For God, I Die. There Is A Camera Outside The Door, And Jesus Is Standing There. He Came Just For You. Searching Just For You. You Were Created As A Special Object Of God's Love.

God Made You So He Could Love You. This Is The Truth That You Should Build Your Life On.

You Are Not A Mistake. You Were Born When God Wanted You To Be, Predestined That Is Who You Are.

A Time Set In Motion For You To Begin Your Life. God Has Plans Just For You. We All Have A Purpose In This Life.

So Stop Running, Catch Your Breath, Breathe, And Now Let Go.

Today Is The Beginning Of the Rest Of Your New Life. What Are You GOING TO Do With It?

Your Race And Your Nationality Are No Accident. He Created You For Himself. You Were Loved Before You Were Even Born. Get This In Your Spirit. You Were Loved Before You Were Even Born.

He Knew You Before You Were In Your Mother's Womb, That Is How Precious You Are To Him.

A Friend Is Always Loyal, And A Brother Is Born To Help In Times Of Need. Jesus Is Your Friend, and He Is Your Big Brother (Proverbs 17:17).

For I Hold You By Your Right Hand—I Am The Lord Your God. And I Say To You, "Don't Be Afraid. I Am Here To Help You."

You Have The Key To Unlock The Door. So What Are You Waiting For? God Has Always Been With You.

And He Always Will Be. You Are Going To Have To Get To the Point In Your Life,

For God, You Will Live; And For God, You Will Die.
The Greatest Love Of Your Life Is In Love With You.
Thank You, My Lord, for Being At My Door.

Love always,
Sister Sugar
MS. Juanita Wilson

Holy Spirit

Holy Spirit, I thank You for being so close to me. There is no separation between You and me.

I didn't understand until today what it really means when Your Word says a Comforter. And that You will lead me into all truth. I understand that the compassion that I have for my brother and sister is because of You. I am reading a book called *The Spirit Contemporary*. And it has changed my life. I never understood how close You are to me until right at this moment, Lord. I thank You for revealing something so wonderful to me. You have helped me understand that You will never leave me or forsake me. This has become so real to me. Thank You, my Lord, for loving me so much that You have given me a piece of You to live with me forever. Thank You so much for caring so much about me and the rest of Your children. Holy Spirit, come and teach me to hear Your voice, to move, and not be afraid. Because You will always be with me. Thank You, Holy Spirit, for always being here with me. To do what is right is a protection for your life.

Thank You for being my friend,
Love Sis. Sugar
Ms. Juanita Wilson

The Eternal Life

You are going to have to believe that Jesus Christ is the Son of our God. You cannot receive eternal life if you don't believe that Jesus is the Son of the Father Who lives in heaven.

Since we have been made right in God's sight by faith, we have peace with God because of what Jesus Christ, our Lord, has done for us. Because of our faith, Christ has brought us to this place of undeserved privilege where we now stand, and we confidently and joyfully look forward to sharing God's glory.

We can rejoice when we run into problems and trials, for we know that they help us develop endurance. And endurance develops strength of character, and character strengthens our confidence and hope of salvation. For we know how deeply God loves us because He has given us the Holy Spirit to fill our hearts with His love.

Christ came at the right time and died for us, sinners. God showed His great love for us by sending Christ to die for us while we were still sinners. And since we have been made right in God's sight by the blood of Christ, He will certainly save us from condemnation. Since our friendship with God was restored by the death of His Son while we were still His enemies, you and I will certainly be saved through the life of His Son. And now we can rejoice in our wonderful new relationship with God because our Lord Jesus Christ has made us friends of our God.

What shall we say about such wonderful things as these? If God is for us, who can be against us? For God Himself has

GIVEN US THE RIGHT STANDING WITH HIMSELF. CHRIST JESUS DIED FOR US AND WAS RAISED TO LIFE FOR US. AND HE IS SITTING IN A PLACE OF HONOR AT GOD'S RIGHT HAND, PLEADING FOR US. OUR OVERWHELMING VICTORY IS OURS THROUGH CHRIST, WHO LOVES US. YOU ARE PART OF ETERNAL LIFE. PLEASE DON'T MISS GOING TO HEAVEN TO BE WITH YOUR GOD.

THE ETERNAL LIFE
THANK YOU, MY LORD
MS. JUANITA WILSON

About the Author

Juanita Wilson is from Shepherd, Texas. Her life has not been easy. She had always known Who God was, but not until she was an adult did she give her life to Christ. From her small beginning, she has emerged as a woman who loves God with all her heart. She has four adult children, grandchildren, and even great-grandchildren. She uses words on paper to express her love for Jesus and as an instrument to give her testimony. She uses artful words to bless the lives of other people. They have become the evangelistic tools that she uses everywhere she goes. Her life's work is for people to fall in love with Jesus, as she has. She is His instrument of righteousness, inviting you to come in and experience this Jesus Who has changed her life. She is a survivor, an overcomer, and a light. She has taken the messes of her life and made them a message to free others from bondage. She has returned from death five times because God has a purpose for her life. Even in her seventies, she continues to dare to dream and be who God created her to be. She is one of those people you will never forget when you meet her. She is the kind of person who will give you her last. Yet her heart continues to be open, and her greatest desire is to share the love of Jesus with everyone. She will make you laugh. She will cry with you during your tough times.

But most importantly, she has the heart to serve others. Juanita Wilson, at her core, is an evangelist of the gospel through poetic poems for the Lord wherever she goes. She allows God to use her gift because she is eternally grateful for what God has done in her life. She completely surrenders to doing His will until He calls her home.